ZILCH
TO
CONVERSATIONAL

A Guide to Quickly Attain Conversational Fluency in Any Language

DANIEL V. RUSTEEN

First edition: July 2019

Cover Design: Tooba Saleem

Interior Layout Design: Heidi Marttila-Losure

Editor: Kris M. Smith

Table of Contents

Hyperlinks

All of the links in this book can be found, by chapter, on my website at www.dannybooboo.com/zilch_to_conversational. Please note that capital letters contained in any links in this book must be capital when entered into your browser.

I. Who is this for?

This book is for English speakers who want to learn to communicate in a foreign language. It is an accelerated method for learning a target language up to the conversationally-fluent level.

I define accelerated learning, in this case, as quickly learning a language *before* learning how to communicate fluently in it. The idea of this guide is to give you options and put some pieces together, so you're equipped to make the right decisions for your individual situation.

The most significant difference between this guide and others is that I'm not claiming to bring you to a completely-fluent level. Why? I don't think it's necessary. The amount of effort it takes to go from 80% fluent to 90% fluent is immense, and anything above 90% fluent is gargantuan. For business-minded readers, the return on investment in terms of time invested for increased fluency shrinks amazingly fast after you reach the 80% fluent mark.

Ask yourself before buying this guide: "Will I be happy communicating with 80% efficiency in my target language?"

If you've heard of the 80/20 rule, or the Pareto Principle, this will make perfect sense to you. The 80/20 rule says that 80% of output is due to 20% of input. This phenomenon is repeated throughout the world. For example, in farming, 20% of the crop produces 80% of the yield; in society, 20% of the population has 80% of the wealth.

We'll be focusing our energy on the 20% of language-learning information that is responsible for 80% of comprehension.

The point of language is to communicate. Although grammar rules are important, they aren't always necessary to get your message across. Whenever you effectively communicate, your mission is accomplished!

What I'm claiming this method will do is this: it will bring you to a basic conversationally-fluent level within 60 days if you invest two hours per day in study. This means:

- Speaking comfortably in common situations (in restaurants, in taxis, negotiating in marketplaces, and basic spontaneous conversation with a stranger)

- Being able to joke around with native speakers and show your personality

- Being able to go on a date, which requires verbal gymnastics and creativity
- Being able to understand native speakers speaking at a normal pace (not during a passionate rant)

You won't be able to:

- Discuss complex subjects (religion, philosophy, politics, etc.)
- Participate effectively in group conversations with native speakers
- Understand rapid speakers
- Understand slang or colloquialisms

II. Introduction to Learning a Language

Hi. I'm Danny. I've made plenty of mistakes on my language-learning journeys. But now I'm fluent in Spanish and at a basic conversational level in Russian. I feel confident this guide will help steer you clear of the mistakes I made and speed up your learning curve.

I tried twice (unsuccessfully) to learn a language. My third attempt was successful.

My first attempt to learn Spanish was in high school, which I probably shouldn't even count. Why the American school system introduces a second language to you in high school when hairs start popping out of your body in unusual places and your libido takes over is a mind-blowing mystery to me. It defies logic. The last thing I wanted to do as a teenager was learn a second language.

My second attempt to learn Spanish occurred in 2011 when I had a real-world office job. I studied

Rosetta Stone for an hour before and after work for about four months.

This, too, was a failure. I lacked motivation. I was learning, but I had no reason to continue as I had no reason to learn the language in the first place. I experience this lack a motivation a second time while I was learning Russian in India. I decided to start learning Russian three weeks before I was in a Russian-speaking country. By the third week, even though I knew I'd need Russian in only one week, I felt my motivation slowly decline. On the flip side, my motivation sky-rocketed when I landed in Almaty, Kazakhstan (Russian is spoken here as the default language) and really wanted to communicate with the locals.

The third attempt—which led to the creation of this guide—began in November 2017 because I was lucky enough to be able to travel to Latin America.

"How long will you stay in Guatemala?" Mom called after me as I rushed to Dad's car so he could drive me to the airport.

"One month!" I yelled back, stuffing myself into the car.

"Hah! C'mon, really!?!" Mom said it with an air of disappointment; she knew I couldn't accomplish my goal in a single month.

To be honest, I knew I would stay longer—I had no return ticket! But I was hopeful I would be conversationally fluent in 30 days.

I was gung-ho. Before I went, I researched where the best place in the world to learn Spanish was. I narrowed it down to Antigua, Guatemala. Antigua is renowned for having a million Spanish schools, an extremely low cost of living, a neutral accent, and a slow speaking pace.

I planned to take four hours of instruction per day and be fluent in a month. I quickly realized the teaching methods were antiquated and too inefficient for me. They were nearly identical to how I failed to learn Spanish in high school, so I quickly realized they wouldn't work for me.

I tried six schools and 13 teachers. I finally found one that was unaffiliated with a traditional school and, although the teacher was the best to date, I knew there was technology I could use to learn even faster and better.

I left Guatemala in March, disappointed that I wasn't yet fluent, but confident in my continued learning. I blamed not being fluent on the fact that too much English was spoken there.

I decided I had to go to a city where no English was spoken, knowing this would *force* me to speak Spanish. THIS is the KEY, I thought.

So, I traveled to Pereira, Colombia, a city with 600,000 inhabitants and no foreigners. But then I realized (much to the delight of folks who cannot travel to the country where their target language is spoken) that it makes no difference where you are in the world. This is especially true for English speakers because English is spoken around the world and the only thing that changes when you go to a smaller city without English is that the people who do speak English want to practice their English on you!

After these experiences, I realized the most important keys to learning any language: You need to set expectations, a motivational force, and a study plan.

I know. It doesn't sound like much. But hold on.

To successfully and efficiently learn a language, **you need to set expectations, a motivational force, and a study plan.**

It makes no difference where you are physically. Though I will say that wanting to communicate with the locals will be a huge and automatic motivational force if you are fortunate enough to travel. If not, you can travel to where your target language speakers congregate in your town.

If you don't create a study plan days and weeks will go by without progress.

It really is that simple.

The caveat here is that you need to know WHAT and HOW to study and how to measure progress to maintain your motivation.

Which is where this guide comes in. I will lay out all your options from my experience. I'm actively learning Russian and I learned Spanish in six countries over nine months via real-life teachers in and out of formal language schools, phone apps, online live teachers, and other online programs. This book is a summary of the techniques I use to learn languages.

Above all, I found it most useful to organize what I learned in a Google document, not by how it was presented to me by external aids, but by how it made sense to me in my own brain. This will help you own the language. To see my example for Spanish, go to www.dannybooboo.com/spanish-language-cheat-sheet.

Some of these options will be mandatory, but most will be your choice. Even if you have just 30 minutes a day, that works out to 182 hours a year.

How much time do you spend on Netflix or Facebook?

If learning a language is something you really want to do, you'll be able to find an average of two hours every day or more. This includes watching Netflix or YouTube with target language subtitles. **You'll need no more than 60 days at two hours per day to become conversationally fluent**[*]. This is because the system will lay out your best study plan to an extremely efficient degree. Then, I'll give you so many options and tools, and different ways to learn, that you'll actually do it.

---

[*]   For Category 1 level languages for English speakers (https://en.wikibooks.org/wiki/Wikibooks:Language_Learning_Difficulty_for_English_Speakers).

Here's what
"just x minutes a day"
look like over 365 days...

5 min/day	30 hrs
10 min/day	60 hrs
15 min/day	91 hrs
20 min/day	121 hrs
30 min/day	182 hrs
60 min/day	365 hrs

Before you start, there's one thing you can do to speed up your learning: **learn English grammar rules**. If you don't know what a direct object is in English, how will you know what it is in your target language? Buy a grammar book and take a week to familiarize yourself with what's in it.

One more thing. **You'll need benchmarks**. I won't mention this again, so pay attention. A benchmark will be one of your motivational prompts. A benchmark is something you can measure as you improve over time. If you were running a marathon, the benchmark would be the time it takes you to run the marathon. Day one, you run it in five hours; six months of training, you run it in three hours. You're able to measure your improvement.

Because this is so important, I'm going to belabor the point.

When was the last time you felt motivated to go to the gym? Maybe you started out going five days per week, but after a few weeks you stopped going. You no longer felt motivated. Do you know why? You lost motivation because you didn't have benchmarks and a plan. You didn't set any expectations.

Without benchmarks, you didn't notice changes or improvements, even though they were there. Had you taken your measurements at the beginning and measured again after two weeks, the changes would have given you additional motivation.

Going to the gym is hard on your body, just as dedicating two hours of your day to learn a new language will be hard on your brain and social life. So, ensure continuing motivation by creating benchmarks!

You can do this any way you want with your target language, but I recommend television. Choose a kid's cartoon and watch it in your target language. Then, two weeks later (if you're studying 4+ hours per day, you can shorten the time to one week) watch the same episode to be amazed by how much more of it you understand.

The above would be a listening-activity benchmark, arguably the most valuable and hardest skill. It is also easy to measure.

You can also set a reading benchmark easily and concretely by buying a book of short stories with chapters of similar length. Record how many words you don't know in one chapter, then revisit the same chapter a month later. If there are multiple choice questions at the end, see how many more you answer correctly the following month. Don't worry about re-reading the same chapter twice; you will have forgotten almost everything within a couple days of reading it the first time. This is because our brains do a good job of throwing out information that they deem useless and with a new language, at first your brain deems it useless. This is an important concept that we'll revisit later, but for now let's play a game.

Tell someone to create a list of 10 words in English and your target language. The words in your target language should be easy for you to pronounce. You can read (or have your friend read to you) the words in English first, then repeat them back immediately. Do the same for the target language words and I can guarantee you'll have remembered many, many more words of English than of your target language. This is because your brain deems the new language useless until you prove to it that the new information is useful. You do this by attaching meaning to the new words and sounds through the techniques in this book.

Overview of Chapters

Here's a quick summary of what's to come. This guide will start slow (parts III and IV). This is because I mention a few tools outside of this book that you'll need to download or learn to effectively learn your target language. Starting in Part V, things will speed up.

Parts III and IV are mandatory. Part III will train your ears—something left completely out of study programs—so you can recognize the new sounds (so your brain doesn't deem them useless). Then it will introduce you to 80% of the vocabulary in your target language via the most frequently used words. Part IV is the system you'll be using for the rest of your language-learning journey and, likely, for other aspects of your life, too. It makes memorizing anything easy.

Part V and VI introduce you to two optional tools, books and teachers. Although they're optional, they're useful. But you cannot simply hire a teacher or buy a book. You need to know where to look and how to choose effectively. You'll find the answers here in this guide.

Part VII takes you through the options you have for working on the four parts of language: speaking, listening, reading, and writing. For example, if you're a music lover, you'll want to use LyricsTrainer, which presents you with a music video and lyrics;

you listen and choose the right words for the missing lyric. Or, if you prefer to learn while meeting people, I'll have you use Tandem, which lets you have conversations with folks around the world and even meet up with some of them in person when they live in your area.

Part VIII is where I'll summarize everything into your personal 60-day summary guide to target conversational language fluency. Essentially, part VIII is a summary of the book and an outline of the plan you'll personalize to your taste and preferences.

Part IX is an introduction to me. Some of this was covered in Part II, but I'll give details about how to get in touch with me.

The final part, X, is where I list additional resources that didn't cleanly fit into any other section of this book, but what you find there should significantly help you achieve your fluency goals if you choose to use them.

Finally, you'll see a Chapter Summary at the end of each part to rehash the most important concepts you just learned. I recommend bookmarking these for later.

Now, before I set you off to the races, remember two additional things during your language-learning process:

- Google is your friend. Any issue you'll have, many people have already had, written about, and developed solutions for, and you should leverage this information.

- Introducing stress to your environment greatly accelerates your learning. Whenever you get that uneasy feeling in your stomach, it's your time to act. In the elevator with a group of target-language native speakers, you'll feel embarrassed to speak to them. This is your body telling you that you ***should*** speak. Promise me that, from now on, you'll interpret the uneasy feeling in your body as an opportunity to accelerate your learning. When you find yourself hesitant, always yield to Action.

One last thing. I'll refer to the following levels you'll pass through to attain conversational fluency:

1. **Absolute Beginner:** You know how to say basic words; you have a vocabulary of less than ten words

2. **Introducer:** You have a set of memorized phrases, questions, and responses for the most common situations (restaurants, taxis, and introductions)

3. **Trickster:** You're able to trick target-language speakers into thinking you're conversationally fluent with strategies and by speaking more complex sentences correctly.

4. **Conversationalist:** You're able to have spontaneous, enjoyable conversations on basic topics

Chapter Summary

▶ To learn efficiently, you need to develop a study plan and set expectations

▶ Create benchmarks, which are yardsticks to measure your improvement. This is important to maintain motivation through the frustrating process of learning a new language

▶ If you aren't already familiar with English grammar, buy a book and read it before you start

▶ You need to commit 2 hours per day of study time for 2 months

▶ Google is your friend; any problem you have has already been solved

▶ Introducing stress to your environment greatly accelerates your learning. When you get that uneasy feeling in your stomach, it's communicating an opportunity to accelerate your learning

III. Beginner's Plan – Train Your Ears First

Learning languages is simple. First, you start with sounds. Then, you move on to words. Last is sentences. Sounds is without a doubt the most important period of your language learning journey.

That is to say, in the first week, you will train your ears to recognize the sounds. I didn't do this at first (because I was unaware of this strategy), but when I did, eight months after I started, it all came together.

My goal for this chapter is to give you a brief introduction and then have the professionals (polyglots who speak 5+ languages) explain more and teach you how to train your ears so you have confidence in the process.

Before I continue, I want to tell you why this is important.

If you don't train your ears first, you'll have a hard time listening (and speaking). This is because your brain filters out unrecognizable sounds. I'm sure you can understand how hard and frustrating it will be to embark on the already-frustrating journey of learning a new language before you've trained your ears (and brain) to recognize new sounds as being valuable.

With trained ears, your vocabulary retention will improve, you'll comprehend faster, and native speakers won't switch to English when you speak with them.

Give yourself a week and do this properly and you'll start with good habits and be rewarded with an accelerated learning curve for the rest of your language-learning journey. During this first week supplement the below training recommendations with YouTube videos on sounds and pronunciation of your target language.

Every language sound in the world is created when you blow air out of your mouth, nose, or both. You create a vowel when you don't put anything in the way (teeth, tongue, etc.). When you put something in the way, or constrict airflow somehow, you create a consonant.

As an absolute beginning step, I want you to watch the following three videos to understand how sounds are made. They'll teach you how to understand pronunciation in your own language so you can apply it to your target language. This is fantastic baseline knowledge for any language you want to learn, and you'll likely come back and re-watch these videos during your language-learning journey.

If you prefer to read first, go ahead and do so; I have assembled in Part VIII all the steps covered in this guide to learn a language in 8-weeks as a quick reference guide for you.

Video One: Consonants 1: Voicing and Place (8:34) (https://www.youtube.com/watch?v=-e66ByetpDY)

SPOILER ALERT (or reminder): Voicing is about whether your vocal cords are vibrating. Compare the word fun (unvoiced) to van (voiced/vibrating). Place is too complicated to explain via text, but it's competently explained in the video; it has to do with what you're doing with your articulators (lips, teeth, tongue, etc.) to make a sound.

Video Two: Consonants 2: Manner and the English Consonants (9:49) (https://www.youtube.com/watch?v=jJR1VPzayu0)

This video is a demonstration of Manner. In the chart, Manner (how much air flow is stopped or impeded) is on the left and Place (placement of articulators in the mouth) is on top. On the top and from left to right, the articulators go from toward the front of your mouth to toward the back. While demonstrating the sounds, he places a neutral vowel sound on both sides. In his case, he says ahhhhhh, as you would say to a dentist. Starting at 7:45, he goes over only the English sounds on this chart. This is important because you'll begin to understand what's going on in your mouth with familiar sounds and you'll more easily be able to correct your own pronunciation with these charts in your target language.

Remember this link as a resource when you start learning the sounds of your target language, as it produces a chart specific to your target language (replace [language] with your target language, for example, Russian or Spanish): www.en.wikipedia. org/wiki/[language]_phonology

Video Three: Vowels: Height, Rounding and Backness (14:28) (https://www. youtube.com/watch?v=eeaghqkLRi8)

This video explains the three elements of vowels: Height, Rounding, and Backness. It introduces a chart that is supposed to mimic the position of the tongue in your mouth. The right column is the Height, the top row is the Backness, and Rounded sounds are on the right-hand side within the chart.

The first step to learning any new language as an English speaker is to understand how the sounds in the English language are made so you can properly identify the differences in other languages and draw sound comparisons. To do this, we must learn the English sounds in the International Phonetic Alphabet (IPA).

The IPA is a sound alphabet; each symbol has one sound, always. Compare this to the English "regular" alphabet which can have many sounds for the same letter. In fact, American English has five vowels symbols to represent 15 vowels sounds!

For example, the 'c' in 'cat' and 'nice' produce different 'regular' alphabet sounds (in this case 'c' in 'cat' is 'k' in IPA and 'c' in 'nice' is 's' in IPA), but only one 'regular' alphabet symbol (i.e. the 'c'). In the IPA, each sound would be represented by a different symbol (i.e. the 'c' in cat and the 'c' in nice will have two symbols, one for each sound).

Alternately, 'Symbol' and 'Cymbal' are spelled differently but sound the same. With the IPA, they would be represented by the same symbol. So, while a symbol in the traditional alphabet represents a letter (which can have multiple different sounds), each symbol in the IPA represents a single sound.

Examine this chart before you continue:

Sound	'Regular' Alphabet	IPA
'C' in **C**at	C	K
'C' in Ni**c**e	C	S
'C' in **C**ymbal	C	S
'S' in **S**ymbol	S	S

Notice how the 'c' in the final three rows all have the same sound. Thus, they have the same IPA symbol ('S'). And the 'c' in 'cat' is represented by a different letter/sound in the IPA. The whole idea of this exercise is to start to understand **how** you are making your English sounds. Right now, you do it automatically and probably have never given any thought to it. But in your new language, you'll need to think about your tongue placement to produce the correct sound so native speakers can understand you.

Watch the following video for an introduction to the English sounds in the IPA: https://www.youtube.com/watch?v=OWJb4ryZwQc

To buy what you see in the above video, Fluent Forever's International Phonetic Alphabet Anki Deck (highly recommended, saves you a bunch of time, we will get into what Anki is later): https://fluent-forever.com/product/international-phonetic-alphabetipa-anki-deck/

If you want to buy the specific pronunciation trainers for your target language (I recommend you do so), you can do that here: https://fluent-forever.com/product/fluent-forever-pronunciation-trainer/

Once you understand what the IPA is, you'll more directly apply it as you start learning your language and have a difficult time with certain sounds.

Minimal pairs are another important step when it comes to training your ears to hear the differences between similar-sounding words. For example, a minimal pair in English would be 'back' and 'bag' or 'free' and 'three'. It is incredibly hard for a non-native speaker to hear the difference between these words without training their ears. Minimal pairs make for a hilarious game with your foreign friends who will have tremendous difficulty pronouncing the subtle difference between any English minimal word pair. (You'll be similarly hilarious in your target language). Minimal pair training is included with the pronunciation trainer above if you decide to buy it. To create minimal pair flashcards:

Step One: Download the Fluent Forever model deck: http://www.fluent-forever. com/wp-content/uploads/2014/05/ Model-Deck-May-2014.apkg

For now, just download it. In the next chapter I'll tell you more about how to setup Anki deck on your computer and phone (it's easy).

Step Two: Follow these instructions: https://fluent-forever.com/gallery/ ear-training-flashcards/

Only after you've trained your ears should you start learning full words. The first step is to start learning the most-frequently-used-words list. Generally, the first 500 words of a language accounts for 80% of the spoken language. This doesn't mean you'll understand 80% of what people say—far from it, but it's a nice idea and a perfect starting point!

I recommend buying Fluent Forever's "The Most Awesome Word Lists You Have Ever Seen" product. It gives you the most frequent 625 words without having to search the internet. This product also organizes the words into themes to help you memorize them.

Link: https://fluent-forever.com/product/most-awesome-word-lists-ever-seen/

If you don't want to buy this list, simply search 'frequency list [target language]' on Google.

Mimic Method

Mimic Method's slogan is 'Learn a foreign language "by ear"'. I found Mimic Method to be very helpful so I'm recommending it to you. Buy and use it as part of your Week One activities.

The system is focused on pronunciation and communication, first and foremost. It takes the conventional system of learning the alphabet and written system first and flips the script.

The goal with Mimic Method, not unlike the one presented in this guide, is to get to caveman speak quickly ('Water...I want', or 'Time...now...what?'). Then refine the speaking as you go.

Additionally, Mimic Method wants you to create a scripted introduction of yourself near the beginning of your studies with near perfect pronunciation. This conditions the native language speaker that you are more fluent than you are and that they can speak to you in the target language rather than switching to English. I think it's ingenious and a combination of our Introducer and Trickster levels.

Last, I want to emphasis a point from the Mimic Method that turned on a light bulb for me. Every language has elemental sounds, the basic building blocks of language. The Mimic Method will teach you these elemental sounds so your brain starts recognizing them. But, in addition to the elemental sounds, the language has sound patterns with distinct sounds that need to be understood. For example, in Spanish, you have the elemental sounds 't' and 'r', but you also have the sound pattern of 'tr' as in 'trabajar'. Taking this a step further, you'll will notice sentence structure patterns, too. These should turn on light bulbs for you during your studies.

I recommend starting with Mimic Method. The service is helpful, affordable, and can be completed in less than a week if you spend a couple hours a day on it.

To learn more and subscribe: http://bit.ly/2LY8J5z

Pimsleur

The Pimsleur method is in the same teaching family as Mimic Method; that is, by ear. The difference is that with Pimsleur it's 100% audio-based. You'll listen to a lecture (no video) and verbally answer questions or repeat words.

This is a very popular system; you can find many reviews online with a simple search. For many learners, Pimsleur is a wonderful option and I recommend you look into it.

Personally, I felt it was way too easy to listen passively; I found myself having to rewind and re-listen to lectures because I started dozing off. And the cost is quite high—in the multiple hundreds of dollars range—depending on your target language.

Chapter Summary

▷ Train your ears via the Mimic Method to help your brain accept new sounds and words as valuable information

▷ Learn about the International Phonetic Alphabet and how it relates to sounds in English and in your target language

▷ Setup Anki on your phone and desktop computer

▷ Buy or create your target language's most-frequently-used-words list in Anki

▷ Create Minimal Pair flashcards in your Anki deck to further train your ears

IV. Spaced Repetition System

The spaced repetition system (SRS) is a beautiful magic trick whose secret I'm going to reveal to you now. Think of SRS as a tool that would have helped you memorize the periodic table of elements or any other seemingly useless information from high school...*easily*. This is SRS. Using SRS, I was memorizing 30 new words every day for days on end in just minutes a day. After nine months, I had a vocabulary of 5,500 words. I know the exact number because that's how many Anki cards I had in my Spanish deck.

SRS is a system of flashcards. Each flashcard is shown to you repeatedly based on how easily you recall the answer for it. Humans have a consistent rate at which we forget new information, so SRS shows you a digital flashcard just before you're most likely to forget it. And it's important when creating your flashcards to associate a sound, imagery, and some personal connection to each word.

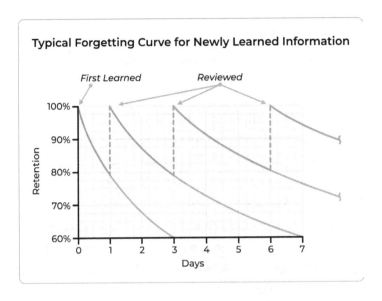

Typical Forgetting Curve for Newly Learned Information

For example, on day one, you'll give the correct answer to your new card. Then, you'll see the same card the next day. If it's easy for you to remember the correct answer, you tell the system, and it will show you the card in two days. If, on the second day, you take a couple seconds to remember the correct answer, the card will be shown to you in another two days. But if you easily remember the word, it would be shown to you in four days (and so on). The more times you remember a word consecutively, the farther into the future the card is pushed before it's shown to you again.

If, after a few rounds, you forget the word, the routine doesn't start from the beginning (Day 1,

Day 2, etc.). Instead, you'll begin seeing it more often until you master it.

An important part of this training relies on honesty. If you immediately remember a word, you'll indicate so by clicking the appropriate button. If you remember the word, but it took you a second, you'll say so. If you remember the word after thinking about it a while, you'll say so. And, if you can't remember the word, you'll say so. There are usually four options to choose from.

Fluent Forever has created a wonderful webpage introducing you to the Anki deck and how to set it up. Please have a look now or bookmark it for later: https://fluent-forever.com/chapter2/

Here's another resource with links and instructions on how to create each type of card: https://blog.fluent-forever.com/gallery/

When everything is set up on your computer and smartphone, you'll be using a few tools to create new cards:

- www.Forvo.com for pronunciations by native speakers

- www.TinyURL.com/BasicImage to add a small image to each card

- https://translate.google.com/ to ensure your spelling is correct (and the auto-correct feature makes adding special symbols easier)

Or, you can use this web tool to automate much of the process for you: https://blog.fluent-forever.com/multi-search/. (Just find your language.)

In case you missed an important rule from the Fluent Forever Anki deck tutorial, here it is again: **One card, one answer**. Don't ask for every month of the year or all conjugations for a single word on one card. And don't make your flashcard generic. (Example: instead of a card that says General Greeting, explain exactly what the greeting is: Good afternoon.)

Regarding the sound you will include on the flashcard, you have two options: you can select the actual word you're learning, or you can select a simple phrase. For example, if you're learning the word 'bocina' in Spanish (it means 'horn'), you can choose to add the pronunciation of 'bocina' or something more like 'tocar la bocina' which means 'honk'. In this way, you've just listened to how 'bocina' is properly pronounced and you picked up some bonus vocabulary. You can use Forvo for pronouncing phrases, but I suggest you use www.rhinospike.com to pronounce entire sentences.

Personally, I discovered that learning 30 new cards per day reached the upper-limit of my brain capacity. Any more, and I'd start forgetting a high percentage of the cards I had learned the day before—and then I'd get frustrated. (Learning any new language is frustrating anyway so I suggest you limit the feeling wherever possible.)

If you're learning more complex grammar rules or words, change your per day new card limit to as few as ten. And focus on the 'I' and 'you' conjugations first because these will be the two you'll be using most at the start. (You won't start referring to others using them and they conjugations until you're more advanced.)

Set your review cards to no more than 200 per day. (These are the cards you've seen and become familiar with in the past that come back around so you don't forget them.)

Just as important as memorizing words is memorizing phrases/patterns. All languages use similar patterns so memorizing them will help your listening comprehension.

Fluent Forever Mobile Application

Gabriel Wyner has been working on a mobile app for Android and iPhone devices since 2017 to incorporate all the principles of the SRS method.

Meant to be an alternative to Anki, it includes sound and pronunciation training, word frequency lists, grammar rules, and conversation practice.

I've used the Beta version for a while and the official app was released in mid-2019. Unfortunately, I do not recommend this app. It's not nearly effective as you creating your own flashcards. And, the grammar section seems ineffective. However, you can give it a go with the free trial.

The cost is $9.99 monthly. Current support languages are Spanish (both Latin America and Spain), French, Russian, Italian, German, Korean, and Portuguese (Brazilian).

To learn more and subscribe: https://fluent-forever.app/

Chapter Summary

▶ SRS is a system of flashcards that helps you memorize new information by showing it to you just before you forget it

▶ Use Forvo, tinyurl.com/basicimage, and Google translator to create your own digital flashcards

▶ As a baseline, learn no more than 30 cards per day (10 if they are complex words or rules) and review no more than 200 per day

▶ Focus on the 'I' and 'You' conjugations first

V. Teachers

A teacher is a nice supplemental, but far from compulsory, tool during your language-learning journey. There are strong arguments both for and against using a teacher. You can teach yourself a lot of the basics more efficiently than most teachers. But there may come a time when having a human teacher to clarify concepts and answer questions in real time becomes efficient and reduces some of the frustration in the process of learning a new language.

The argument for a (good) teacher is that you'll learning exactly what you need and when you need it. That's easier said than done as many teachers are not good. Another pro of having a teacher is accountability. If you have a daily class scheduled (and you're paying for it) you're more likely to show up. Finally, a teacher should be able to provide additional material based on what you are learning. This saves you both time and money. However, I find that high-quality content that is thoughtfully and logically created often has a better structure.

If you're a beginner, your teacher **must** speak fluent English. If you're choosing your own teacher, this is easy to verify. It gets complicated when schools insist that if you're learning a new language you should learn in that language. I tried this; it doesn't work. What happens (beyond extreme frustration) is an hour-long class to teach you a concept that could be taught in English in five minutes and mastered in 55 simply by practicing it.

When you find a teacher that works for you, create a specific schedule on day one. You need to have a plan to know what you'll learn and when. If the teacher is hesitant to do this or launches into her regular plan as she does with every student, find a new teacher who understands you're a unique student with individual needs and reasons for learning the target language. Bad teachers will endeavor to retard your progress because their income is based on how slowly you learn new concepts (hmm, teachers who insist on only speaking in target language no matter your level...).

A plan matters a lot on your journey. A plan is necessary because you'll need measuring sticks along the way and a plan is a great measuring stick.

Plans also ensure that you aren't learning too much, too fast. I realized this far too long after starting my language-learning journey. If you recall, I took four hours of Spanish class every day. I was learning new concept after new concept without much practice. I was also starting an online business, trying to learn to dance salsa, and living with a Guatemalan family, all of which had their own demands on my time. I realized later that the thing that suffered was actual practice. You need to practice everything you learn, many times over, before moving to a new concept. New concepts are the foundation stones for everything that comes later in your journey.

Your language teacher won't make you fluent in an efficient manner. This is because language teachers speak *for* students: slowly, clearly, grammatically correct, and without slang. Some of your formal teaching time should be having regular conversations with various people. The protocol and tendency in formal language-learning settings is to talk about the same things using the same sentence formations to the same person. To avoid this, decide on different subjects per day. Here's an example:

Day 1: talk about activities you engaged in last week

Day 2: talk about sports you enjoy watching or doing

Day 3: talk about relationships

Day 4: talk about diet and exercise

Day 5: talk about spirituality

Day 6: talk about politics

Day 7: summarize a recent book you've read

If you're lucky enough to be in your target language country (or can find a local community), structure a class around going into the real world and starting conversations with strangers. This will add stress and accelerate your learning process.

Alternate plan with your teacher: Go through your frequently-used-words list with your tutor and come up with relevant sentences and pronunciations. Fluent Forever describes this plan here: https://blog.fluent-forever.com/italki-tutor-guide/

Also be very clear with your teacher about how fluent you want to get. At one extreme, if you want someone to think you're a native, you'll want the teacher to correct your pronunciation (to the nth degree) and sentence structure. For example, Spanish speakers use the phrase 'in this moment' a lot while speaking English because in Spanish they use the word phrase 'en este momento' a lot. But English-speaking natives don't use the phrase 'in this moment' ever; we say, "Right now." So, even though phonetically you will sound like a native, using 'in this moment' will give you away.

On the other end, you can simply tell the teacher to stop you if you really botch a word or your sentence structure doesn't make sense without significant interpretation on the listener's end. This is important because most teachers won't do this unless they're prompted and reminded.

Here are two tools I recommend and have used:

www.iTalki.com

Starting at $5 per hour and up, you can have one-on-one language lessons with a native speaker. This platform allows anyone to teach, so if you want a formal grammar lesson, you'll pay more to speak with a formal teacher. But, if you just want to practice conversations, you can pay any teacher or native speaker on iTalki to talk with you. I've used this platform to practice conversations and found the teachers to be of high quality. Try turning off your video and using audio alone. Removing visual cues ensures that your teacher will focus solely on your speaking abilities.

Fluent Forever Tutoring Beta App

This tool is super useful for getting recordings from your teacher. Essentially, it is a text box that can be modified by two keyboards, live. When a sentence is agreed upon, have the native speaker say it while recording the audio for your Anki deck. (Read the Fluent Forever tutorial (https://blog.fluent-forever.com/tutoring-tool-beta/) if this instruction isn't immediately clear to you.)

Chapter Summary

▶ Classroom learning with a teacher won't make you fluent

- ▶ At the Absolute Beginner and Introducer level, your teacher **must** speak fluent English

- ▶ If your teacher is online, try audio-only classes to remove visual cues

- ▶ Create a specific schedule for the entire process on day one

- ▶ Make sure you practice every new concept you learn before moving on

- ▶ I recommend using Italki to find a teacher and the Fluent Forever Tutoring app

VI. Books

Books will speed your learning process by giving you an extra 10-20 minutes of learning time every day, at a minimum. I read for 5-10 minutes upon waking and before going to bed most nights of the week. Twenty minutes per day, multiplied by one month, is ten hours of bonus study time.

First up should be a grammar book. However, if you find and prefer to use a good teacher (refer to part V) you won't need a grammar book. (If you have a good teacher but you're still struggling, a grammar book can offer the additional touchpoint you need to commit a rule to memory.)

Remember, the more touchpoints you have with a word, the more connections your brain makes, and the easier it will go into long-term memory to make recalling it easier when you're speaking. If you decide to forgo a teacher, definitely buy a grammar book and create digital flashcards by creating sentences based on the grammar rule you're learning. (For example, here is my flashcard to learn third person present perfect in Spanish: Él les [ha dicho] a todas las respuestas.) Avoid unnecessary flash-cards by creating ones only for rules that are most relevant to you at the time of reading. At first, err on the side of too few flashcards. I ended up deleting a bunch because the grammar rule in question was so rarely used that it made no sense to spend time learning it.

A phrase book is a great idea for two reasons. The first reason is that you can fake fluency faster and extend conversations with target language speakers for longer periods. If you speak a phrase less commonly used by foreigners (or a phrase commonly used incorrectly), you'll signal to the native speaker that you're more fluent than you are. They won't know you just memorized the sentence or question. The second reason is that you'll start understanding that even though the same ideas are communicated in all languages around the world, the way they're communicated differs. For example, to communicate your age in English you say, "I **am** 30 years old", but in Spanish you'd say, "I **have** 30 years" (Yo tengo trenta años). The words used to communicate similar ideas can be very different in other languages. Once you internalize this, it will greatly help you understand and speak to your target language.

A third category could be a book of **short stories**. I bought two of these while learning Spanish (and read one, twice) because I felt they could fill

10-minute gaps easily throughout the day for bonus study time.

When you start searching for books in your target language, you're going to find a bunch of unique and niche books to choose from.

Amazon is going to be your best option for books. As a basic initial search go with "learn [target language]". You can further specify with searches like "[target language] for beginners", "conversational [target language]", etc. Don't overcomplicate it. Open only books with titles and covers that catch your attention. Then, read the table of contents and the book summary to make your final decision. Buy only those books that excite you to open them.

For example, with some digging, I found "Understanding Spanish Conversation: Learn The Words, Phrases, and Grammar Spanish Speakers Use Every Day and Quickly Become One Yourself!" which introduces readers to the subtle differences in meaning of common and related words. It was somewhere between a phrase book and a dictionary.

A special shout out to Fluent Forever by Gabriel Wyner. Buy it!

In addition to **Fluent Forever**, a wonderous book, I also bought and read Fluent in 3 Months by Benny Lewis. Don't buy it. Nothing against Benny Lewis—he obviously knows how to learn a language—but I found his book to be 90% fluff and a waste of time.

Chapter Summary

▶ Books are optional

▶ The types of books you can buy general-ly fall into **grammar** or **phrase/conver-sational** books. A third category is story books.

▶ Phrase books can be very useful for show-ing how familiar sentences are said in your target language to reach the Trickster level

▶ Reading 5-10 minutes before bed and upon waking creates a strong connection in your brain

VII. Skills

There are four skills you must acquire in any language: speaking, listening, writing, and reading. (And there's a fifth, too: thinking.) Force yourself to think in your target language. It's akin to free conversation practice while you walk and do other things. Bored? Have an internal dialogue with yourself in your target language.

Tell yourself what you are doing during your morning routine. The more details the better. If you're at home, you can kill two birds with one stone by speaking out loud what you are thinking (I am brushing my teeth, I just finished eating my eggs and bacon, etc.). When you get stuck, write it down to look up later or discuss with a native speaker or your teacher. Yes, thinking in your target language does count towards your two-hour daily goal.

We'll cover the first four skills now. All four are important but speaking and listening are more important than writing and reading.

Start off with a Google search 'language tools [target language]' to get specific resources for your situation. The resources below apply to all the common languages (and many less-common languages), but there are many great tools made for only one language. For example, if you're learning Spanish you can find awesome services and conversation practice at www.BaseLang.com for very cheap.

This is important and, luckily, fun. It's amazing the quantity of resources (many are free) available on the internet but only for one language. You don't want to miss these. Take an hour to search and click on only those resources that grab your attention. I guarantee that you will find a few that you're truly excited to start using.

Before we jump in further, I must comment on phone apps. They're great and fun but they aren't efficient when it comes to teaching new concepts. I recommend using them ONLY to reinforce what you've already learned or if you have a couple minutes to spare while waiting for the bus. Some of the most common apps are Duolingo, Busuu, and Memrise.

And, a quick shout out to All Language Resources. The guy has reviewed a ton of language-learning resources. I recommend you use it to investigate any resource you are unsure about and to discover new resources.

Speaking

Obviously, you'll want to find conversation partners. This is easy to do, and you don't have to fly to another country to do it. Use the following resources to find conversation partners:

- **www.italki.com:** Website or phone app

- **Tandem:** This phone app is awesome! Connect with people around the world to chat with who are native speakers of your target language. You can communicate with text, voice, or video. You can also search by location to meet up in person.

- **HelloTalk:** Similar to Tandem

- **Language exchanges on Facebook or Meetup.com**

- **www.couchsurfer.com:** Message anyone in your location and ask to meet them. Let them know your intentions up front—that you're interested in practicing your target language. In exchange, buy them a coffee or meal. If all goes well, you'll even make a friend!

- **Speak with local street vendors** (then buy something!)

Here are some tips I picked up during my language-learning journey in the speaking skill department:

- Avoid saying, 'I don't understand' at all costs. This will stop a conversation cold. Anything that tells the speaker it's useless for them to continue speaking because you don't understand, you want to avoid. Instead, say anything else. Literally, anything. Ideally, you can say something that is at least partially relevant to the conversation at hand. (This sounds simpler than it is. Conversation is a funny thing: it can be interpreted in various ways and proceeds on an unpredictable path. Although the target language speaker might think you're speaking randomly, it's important to continue the conversation.)

- Phase out hand gestures; these give the listener clues about what you're saying. Instead, focus on pronunciation so you can make sure your words are correct enough to achieve effective communication.

- Send a voice text message instead of writing one whenever possible. You must think faster when speaking, so it's harder to do this. Since spoken skills are more important than written skills, speak as many messages as you can as often as you can.

- As you achieve 'Trickster' level, start writing down the sentences you think of in your target language but can't convey verbally. Go over them with your teacher or target language speaking partner. (Doing this before you've reached Trickster level will cause too much disruption in your conversations because you'll have to write down too many sentences.) One caveat: do your best to communicate what you want, but are having trouble saying, using other words you know. If you can do this, don't write the sentence. After all, the goal of language is to communicate and if you're able to get your desired point across, even if it takes a little longer, mission accomplished!

Games

Here are some of my favorite games, in order of difficulty level, to play with your target language friend in your target language:

Back Writing

This is a favorite of mine because I can actually feel my brain working and thinking in new ways. It's a two-player game. Player One will write out a word in the target language on player Two's back, one letter at a time. Player Two must guess the word based on Player One's writing. Again, the more connections you have with a word, the more likely it will be pushed into long-term memory. Thus, I recommend using common words for this game.

Murder, Marry, Shag

This is a two-player game. One player goes at a time. Player One will pick three nearby people. Player Two needs to decide which of the three chosen people he will murder (just a game, folks!), marry, and shag (copulate with). And, most importantly, why!

Eye Spy

This is a classic and can be played with unlimited players. Player One will look around and choose an object. Then, he or she will describe what the item looks like and/or where it is without giving away the actual item, using as much or as little detail as needed to elicit the correct response. (Player One, do not look at the item in mind while describing it!) The other players will take turns asking questions and making guesses about the object Player One has chosen.

Five Questions

This is a two-player game. Player One will explain the rules: Player One will ask player two five questions. To win, Player Two must answer all five questions wrong. (Yes, wrong. Incorrectly!) Player One, wait for the confused look on Player Two's face to disappear, then answer Player Two's questions. Your answer will always be: "Yes, incorrectly. Like you're lying to me." (The downside to this game is that it's only playable once per person. You will see why shortly.)

I'm always Player One and I have NEVER lost this game. I'll show you how. But first, here's an example of the game:

> **Example question:** Who is the author of this guide?
>
> **Example answer:** If Player Two answered anything other than Daniel Rusteen, Player Two would have a score of 1 and Player One will ask the second question.

Here's the wrinkle in this game. Player One will ask three questions. In between question one and two, Player One will make a simple comment, like 'good' or 'see, that wasn't so hard'. After question three, Player One will make a slightly longer comment, then pause briefly, and ask Player Two nonchalantly, "What question are we on?" At this point Player Two will usually answer "4" at which point they will have lost and you can let them know. But in about 20% of cases, Player Two will be sharp and say something other than 4. In this case, Player One needs to act super surprised and quickly and surprisingly respond by asking, "Have you played this game before!?!". At this point, 100% of the time, Player Two will answer by excitedly saying "No!". Since that's the fifth question, Player Two answered truthfully, so Player One wins!

The Cube

This is a more advanced two-person game and should not be played before the Trickster level. It's a personality quiz and a fan favorite. Explain to Player Two that you're going to give them a personality test by asking a series of questions. At the end, Player One will reveal to Player Two what their answers mean.

First, explain that you're going to ask Player Two a set of questions and they need to imagine everything in their brain and to tell Player One what they see in their brain. Here are the questions, in order:

1. Picture a cube. How big is the cube?

2. Can you see through the cube or not?

3. If they cannot see through the cube, what color is the cube?

4. Are you looking at an edge of the cube or one of the smooth sides?

5. Picture a ladder in this scene and tell me where, in relation to the cube, it is. (If Player Two needs help, ask them to tell you if the ladder is learning against the cube or not, or maybe on a wall to the side?).

6. Picture a storm in this scene. Where is the storm in relation to the cube and how big is it?

7. On the ground are flowers. How many? Then, what color?

8. Picture a horse standing on the ground. Describe the horse with three adjectives.

At this point, after asking all the questions and after seven to ten minutes of play, I'll usually say "I made everything up and none of it means anything. After the laughs, I'll reveal the answers:

1. If the cube is on the smaller side (human-sized) you can say it represents Player Two's ego (no one wants a big ego). If it's on the larger size (Paris Hilton answered with 'a hotel!'), it can represent self-confidence or self-image. (The players think highly of themselves, or they like themselves).

2. If the cube is transparent, Player Two doesn't have many walls or a guard. People can get to know them easily. If the cube is opaque, they're guarded, and it takes more time for people to get to know them or for them to reveal themselves to new people.

3. The color of the cube is usually their favorite color.

4. If Player Two says they're facing the edge, they're visionaries or entrepreneurial types. If they're facing a smooth side, this is the standard answer (90% of folks say this). It

means they want a more predictable job and life.

5. The ladder represents Player Two's career. The nearness of the ladder to the cube represents how intertwined Player Two is with their job. It doesn't necessarily mean they love their job, but if the ladder is leaning again the cube, the job and Player Two are very involved. If the ladder is on the wall to the side of the scene, it is just a job and Player Two doesn't care about it.

6. The storm represents inner/personal issues. The bigger the storm, the bigger the issues. If the storm is above the cube, Player Two is currently dealing with personal issues. If the storm is in front of or in back, then the player will be facing issues soon or has faced issues in the past, respectively. If the storm is to the side, they are being dealt with concurrently, but not as intensely.

7. The number of flowers can be family/friends or children. The color will usually be their favorite color.

8. The horse—the grand finale and usually very accurate—represents Player Two's ideal mate. A horse is usually described as big, loyal, white or brown, strong, happy, attractive, or stallion.

Listening

Netflix

As a proactive language learner, Netflix will become your favorite new hobby. Buy a subscription and start watching. Sometimes you'll want to watch in your target language and other times in English. For example. sometimes you'll put on Spanish subtitles and other times subtitles in English. Here is a progression you can take:

1. Native language with target language subtitles

2. Target language with native language subtitles

3. Target language with target language subtitles

4. Target language without subtitles

You need to acknowledge and abide by your current level of understanding. At the Introducer level, you might be able to watch cartoons in your target language with target language subtitles, but as you progress, you'll go for more 'adult' series in your target language with native language subtitles.

In general, you want to avoid comedy until you're past the Conversationalist level. Why? Do you get 100% of comedy in your native language? Probably not. You'll understand significantly less comedy in your target language because there's a lot of cultur-ally-centered jokes which you won't be privy to.

Read a summary of what you're about to watch before you watch it. This will help you devote less brain energy to keeping up with the plot and more brain energy to understanding the words. To improve your reading skills, read the summary in your target language before you watch.

LyricsTraining App

I forget how I discovered this delectable app, but it's wonderful. It will show you a music video on the screen with lyrics underneath. The lyrics will move on the screen in accordance with the video and you'll have to guess some of the words (multiple-choice style) based on the difficulty you've chosen. At the end, you'll get a score and be compared to others learning your target language. At the time of this writing, the following languages are available:

- Spanish
- French
- German
- English
- Portuguese
- Italian

It also serves as a nice break during conversational practice.

YouTube

Type into Google "popular YouTube videos in [target country name]" and continue down the rabbit hole. If it's music videos you're after, eventually try to sing along! To increase your reading comprehension (and enjoyment of the song), look up the lyrics. And look up videos with dual translations that show target and native language translations on the screen side by side. It's awesome!

Music adds benefit by connecting emotions to words. The more synaptic connections you can make, the easier remembering words and phrases will be. Be ready to learn slang. (I learned in this way that 'pa' is short for 'para', one of the most frequently used words in Spanish).

You'll find a ton of free (and short) listening activities. I consider these activities fun and easily digestible. The best ones ask a series of questions at the end to test your comprehension. Active learning beats out passive learning every time. Eventually, you'll want to turn off the subtitles and speed up the video to 1.5x.

Other Tips

- As an absolute beginning, listen for gaps between words/syllables instead of meaning as a first step toward actively listening. (Expressed differently, try to identify when one word ends and the next begins. This is the melody or rhythm of the language.)

- Add the Video Speed Controller Chrome extension (https://chrome.google.com/webstore/detail/video-speed-controller/nf-faoalbilbmmfgbnbgppjihopabppdk/related?hl=en) to make video playback easy. This will let you go back, forward, slow down, speed up, or pause a video with the click of a button.

- News, if you can stomach it, makes for a great listening activity because of the lack of slang and simple sentences.

- Podcasts. Obviously. There is boundless free content on any of these apps. In addition to the standard podcast apps, give Stitcher Radio a try (https://www.stitcher.com/).

Writing

Given that we're all addicted to our cell phones, I find the skill of writing easily attained through messaging apps alone. You don't even need a plan for this one. In the process of living life, you'll have to communicate via messages. Just make a conscious effort to do so in your target language. (Avoid using google translate; it can quickly become a crutch that you don't want start relying on.)

Force yourself to actively read for comprehension when you get a message in your target language. I find that an extra reading or two often reveals its meaning. Then, and only then, do I allow myself to use google translate.

Do the same with your messages. First make a concerted effort to type in your target language before relying on google translate. (To reiterate, using a translator is passive learning; the more active learning you do, the quicker you'll learn. In the beginning it will take longer, but it will more than compensate you later when you no longer need to use a translation app. Be patient with yourself. You didn't learn to walk or read or at warp speed. You shouldn't expect to acquire a new language any faster.)

When you're using social media—for example, the stories feature on Instagram—write the text in your target language. When I post a story, I'll post it in English and Spanish. This keeps me at least semi-connected to my friends who only speak Spanish while I'm on the other side of the world (as I am right now while writing this guide). Plus, if I make a mistake, I always get a few messages from friends letting me know how to correct it. (This is a great way to maintain relationships and get free tutoring at the same time!)

Think about keeping a journal. I have kept a journal since I was in 7th grade (that's 20 years of consistent writing, folks!) and I've written in it at least monthly. Maybe that's why this is my third published book. I find journaling therapeutic and recommend writing it in your target or native language. But don't start one in your target language until you're at Introducer level. To make it easier, you can start by answering a question every day. For example, "What is your study plan today?" Write it out in your target language.

Reading

Reading fictional stories will be frustrating, especially if you prefer to read non-fiction. It will be frustrating because your comprehension will be low, and you won't be learning anything except your target language. But hang in there. Reading is an activity you can do for ten minutes at a time upon waking up and just before bed and by committing to it, you'll have a bonus 10 hours of study at month's end.

When choosing a book, find one with short stories that you can read in 5 to 10 minutes. The best books will have a short summary at the beginning and a series of multiple-choice questions at the end. Some will have a list of words which the author assumes you may not know. If it does, read the list before you read the story, even if the list is shown at the end of the story. (It makes no sense to learn a word after you have read the story it appears in, but this is where the word list usually appears.) Some books will have a target language paragraph immediately followed by a native language translation. If this is the case, it's easy to passively read the target language paragraph and then rely on the native language paragraph as a crutch. Only use this crutch *after* you've made a concerted effort to understand the paragraph.

To improve your learning curve, buy the same book as an audiobook and listen along while you're reading. But again—don't listen passively! Actively listen to every word. Don't be afraid to read/listen to the same chapter two or three times. Just like watching a movie or reading a book in your native language multiple times, new things will be discovered. In the case of a book, these "new things" will make neural connections which will make the words and learning "stickier" inside your brain.

At the Trickster level, change your phone's language to your target language. You also can do this with your web browser, Facebook, Netflix, etc.

A word of caution: choosing the wrong things to read is deadly. I chose a newspaper as my first reading experiment and gave up after three days of agony. It was too dry and boring. I simply wasn't interested in reading about the latest series of car thefts or some dude who burned down a building.

I want to highlight, again, how easy (and counterproductive) it is to rely on google translate. If it becomes a crutch, it will slow your reading comprehension tremendously. The worst part is, you won't really notice. You'll think you're doing great. It takes active and constant policing yourself to learn a new language. The benefits are worth it!

(Don't get me wrong, google translate is fantastic; I have it on my favorites bar. It shares that bar with just three other apps on my phone. Its usefulness is undeniable. Just don't let it become a crutch!)

Conclusion

The last thing you'll do is take your favorites from the above lists and make a single list. Your new list will have all the ways you enjoy studying. There will be some days when you just don't want to study and your study plan for the day will be too difficult to get through. On those days, don't force yourself. Instead, consult your list; one of the things listed will pop out to you as being doable on your off day. Here is an example list:

- Go to target language destination and converse with them
  - For example, if you're in the target language country, go to the tourist area to talk with locals or to the local burrito shop (if you're learning Spanish) during off hours (ideally)
- Watch TV or Netflix
  - documentaries, cartoons, sitcoms, etc.
- Watch YouTube

- ○ Either short conversation practice lessons or time-killing videos in target language

- Listen to a podcast

- Read a target language short story from your book

- Extra Anki deck study cards
  - ○ You can also create new flashcards

- Read from your grammar book

- Write extra in your journal

- Complete one song on LyricsTrainer

- Start one conversation with a new partner on Tandem

- Complete one lesson on your favorite app

Chapter Summary

▶ There are four main skills (speaking, listening, reading, and writing) plus thinking that you need to focus on

▶ Phone apps can serve as gap fillers throughout the day, but they don't do a good job of teaching new concepts

▶ Here are your options for improving your speaking skills: iTalki, Tandem, HelloTalk, Couchsurfer, street vendors, games

- ▶ Listening skill activities: Netflix, LyricsTraining, YouTube, Podcasts
- ▶ Texting as you normally do will take care of your writing skill; just remember to not consult your translation app immediately
- ▶ Reading skill activities: short stories, grammar or phrase books, changing phone and browser to target language
- ▶ If you read a short story book, also buy the audio book to listen to at the same time

VIII. Your Zilch to Conversational 8-Week Study Plan

If you recall in Part II where I was revealing my unsuccessful previous attempts to learn a language, you'll realize why it's essential to create a study plan. I'm going to give you a study plan based on this guide and I'm going to work in enough flexibility for you to modify it based on your needs. In other words, it's time to put everything together so you have a process that will help you reach your target language fluency goal. Here goes:

Preparation

- Optional: Read an English grammar book if your native grammar skills are poor.

- Every Day: Create Anki cards as needed and studying existing cards up to 2 hours daily.

- To Beta test the Fluent Forever app mentioned in Part IV: https://fluent-forever.app/

- For a list of all the referenced (and some extra) Fluent Forever tools: https://blog.fluent-forever.com/language-resources/

Level: Absolute Beginner

Week One (Sounds)

1. Watch videos on the IPA and how sounds are made in general (~1 hour)

    o Video One: Consonants 1: Voicing and Place (https://www.youtube.com/watch?v=-e66ByetpDY)

    o Video Two: Consonants 2: Manner and the English Consonants (https://www.youtube.com/watch?v=jJR1VPzayu0)

    o Video Three: Vowels: Height, Rounding and Backness (https://www.youtube.com/watch?v=eeaghqkLRi8)

2. Create your listening benchmark

3. Learn and setup Anki (~1 hour)

    o Full Instructions: https://blog.fluent-forever.com/chapter2/

    o If you buy one of the products below, instructions are included in the manuals. It's easy.

4. Buy English IPA Anki Deck and memorize (~1 hour)

    o https://fluent-forever.com/product/international-phonetic-alphabetipa-anki-deck/

5. Buy pronunciation trainer and memorize (~1 hour)
   - https://fluent-forever.com/product/fluent-forever-pronunciation-trainer/

6. Create minimal pairs Anki cards (~1 hour)
   - Included with pronunciation trainer if bought above

7. Train Your Ears (~10 hours)
   - Complete Mimic Method
   - Supplement with YouTube videos on pronunciation and sounds

Week Two (Words)

1. Create Anki cards for the most frequently used words (~15 hours)
   - Buy: https://fluent-forever.com/product/most-awesome-word-lists-ever-seen/
   - Or, search 'frequency list [target language]'

Level: Introducer

Week Three (Grammar)

1. Find a teacher on www.italki.com or read a basic grammar book (up to 15 hours)
   - Learn basic grammar and language fundamentals

2. Optional: reading benchmark

Week Four (Conversation)

1. Start watching YouTube videos or Netflix (up to 5 hours)
   - Download: Video Speed Controller Chrome extension (https://chrome.google.com/webstore/detail/video-speed-controller/nffaoalbilbmmfgbn-bgppjihopabppdk/related?hl=en)

2. Find a conversation partner (up to 5 hours)

3. Tandem, Hello Talk, or language exchanges

4. Get a teacher to speed your learning of basic grammar and language fundamentals (1 hour)

Level: Trickster

Week Five

1. Conversation (up to 5 hours)
2. Choose a study activity for 1 or 2 of the skills (up to 10 hours)
3. Optional: buy a phrase book
4. Optional: listen to podcasts

Week Six

1. Conversation (up to 5 hours)
2. Choose a study activity for 1-2 of the skills (up to 10 hours)
3. Optional: buy a book of short stories

Level: Conversationalist

Week Seven

1. Change phone and/or browser to target language
2. Conversation (up to 10 hours)
3. Choose a study activity for 1 or 2 of the skills (up to 5 hours)

Week Eight

1. Consciously think in your target language throughout the day
2. Conversation (up to 15 hours)

Study Activities by Skill

- **Speaking:** iTalki, Tandem, Hello Talk, Couchsurfer, Street Vendors, Language Exchange, Games, WhatsApp Voice Messages
- **Games:** Back Writing, Five Questions, Eye Spy, Murder/Marry/Shag, The Cube
- **Listening:** Netflix, LyricsTraining, YouTube, Podcasts/Stitcher Radio
- **Writing:** Journal, Texting
- **Reading:** Grammar book, phrase book, short stories, audio book
- **Phone Apps:** Duolingo, Memrise, Busuu

IX. Introduction to the Author

So...how was it (*big smile*)?!? I'm truly interested in knowing what you think of my strategy. Please share your feedback with me about this guide and your language learning journey.

I'm Danny. I lived 29 years in northern California until I was 'awakened' to learn my first foreign language (Spanish) to a conversationally-fluent level.

I first had the opportunity to learn Spanish in high school. You read how *that* turned out earlier. In a nutshell, I failed.

But, I don't count it as a true failure on my part. I'm assigning failure to the system, not to myself. Who's idea was it to introduce learning a language to a kid just as he transitions from the relative pre-pubescent comfort of middle school to the hormonal awakening that occurs in high school? When guys start getting random hairs popping out all over their bodies and gals start developing breasts, when both are interested in the opposite sex, pop culture, and games more than in learning a new language?

Very literally the last thing I wanted to do in high school was learn a new language! I was more focused on the next time I'll get the chance to see a female on the campus of my all-male, uber-religious high school!

I tried to learn Spanish again after college. I bought Rosetta Stone and studied a bit in the morning before work and in the evenings before bed. I did this for four months until I knew I'd be going in to the Army. Even had I continued, I probably would have failed because I had no one to practice with. Realistically, at the time I didn't *need* to know Spanish. I wasn't interested in Mexican food, salsa dancing, or Latin culture.

Trying to learn a language without establishing a specific goal will waste a lot of your unrecoverable time.

In 2015 I was fired from Airbnb, which led me to where I am today, a much happier, more well-rounded individual. A year later, I started an online business. Unbeknownst to me at the time, this business would allow me to travel the world while working remotely.

Through a series of realizations and conversations, I bought a ticket to Australia on January 9, 2017 for a departure on January 27, 2017. I stayed for three months. I discovered that working for myself gave me a whole bunch of free time!

After a three-month stint back in California to wrap up my affairs and sell or give away 90% of my stuff, I left for Europe. I eventually made my way to Guatemala with the specific goal of learning Spanish. Anyone who has ever been to Guatemala City knows what I'll say next: it's not the best place to learn a language. There are no language schools!

Nevertheless, I learned the 600 most commonly used words in Spanish. This accounts for 80% of spoken language, they told me, so I must be 80% fluent, I figured! What a cinch! After living in Guatemala City for a month and a half, I traveled to Antigua, Guatemala and moved into a home with a local family.

I learned two things there: First, the home's five rooms were filled with other language exchange students! Someone from the family would come over to cook meals for us and chat during the meals but that was it. This was hardly my definition of immersion. Second, I realized I was far from 80% fluent with my 600 most commonly used words; I was more like 5% fluent. My confidence was immediately shattered.

During the next 9 months, I learned Spanish in five countries (Guatemala, Costa Rica, Panama, Colombia, and Mexico). I did self-study, one-on-one study, group classroom study, and formal education at a college university. I lived by myself in Costa

Rica, Panama, and Mexico City, with a local Spanish-speaking family (and 5 children) in Guatemala, and in a dorm-style house in Colombia.

I sped through the first two and a half months learning rapidly with 4 hours of private class daily during the week, slowed for the next 3 months as I discovered Colombia and tried self-study, and then sped up the last 3.5 months while trying a handful of online resources and books (as outlined in this guide).

I didn't go about learning Spanish in an *effective* way, but I did learn a lot, and, more importantly, I spent a lot of time figuring out how everyone else learned foreign languages. Because of my language-learning curiosity, I found all these tools, and blended my formal strategy for learning any language from absolute beginner to conversationally fluent in as efficient a way as possible.

These days, I move every month to a new city, and I do my best to learn as much of the local language as possible. I'm currently in Thailand and I've learned enough to set myself apart from 95% of tourists in just two weeks. (This is less impressive than it sounds. Because Thai is considered a hard language, it's even difficult to say hello and thank you to the untrained ear, so 90% of tourists don't bother learning Thai at all!)

My next language will be Russian. I chose it because it's a useful language in many countries I visit (goal = acquired) and it has a totally different alphabet which will force me to start from Step One, the Absolute Beginner stage. This guide, and your learning, are always a work in progress. I'm sure I'll have an update with improvements and additions toward the end of my 2-month Russian language learning journey.

If you'd like to get in touch, here's where to find me:

- Instagram @DannyBooBoo0
- Facebook at Danny Vroman Rusteen
- The web at www.DannyBooBoo.com

And, please don't forget to leave a review. It will help tremendously. If you've ever written a book, no further explanation is needed. If you haven't, the value of a review is immeasurable. If I could choose a review or the price of this guide in cash in my pocket, I would choose the review.

Thank you.

X. List Of Most Frequent Words + Phrases

Here is a list of words and phrases you can add to your Anki deck to approach the Introducer level and beyond.

Remember, the more connections you can build in your brain for a word, the easier it will be to remember. Every word you know in English has so many connections that you will never forget the language. It's why saying a bad word in a foreign language seems easier– because it doesn't hold any meaningful connections to us...yet.

The below list is in rough order of when you should learn the word. It's also going to be a generic list. Understand that some words are going to be more relevant to you than they are to me.

For example, I learn how to say carbohydrate, protein, fat, and calories rather quickly because I cook and want to read the nutritional labels. But,

I've left those off the below list as they're more relevant to me personally. I also learn names of muscles because I go to the gym and can better ask a question about a particular exercise if I can direct the trainer's attention with my words and movements.

How do you find your personally relevant words? In the course of the day, take note of anything you want to say or read, but cannot. Add the translation to a translation app that keeps records and add those words to your Anki deck every few days.

- [ ] Hello
- [ ] Thank you
- [ ] Bye
- [ ] Please
- [ ] Yes and No
- [ ] Good morning/afternoon/evening
- [ ] Water
- [ ] Good or bad
- [ ] This or that
- [ ] Bill or check
- [ ] Big and small
- [ ] Cool (usually there is a slang way to say this)
- [ ] Coffee
    - American, espresso, latte, etc.

- ☐ Bag
  - As you would ask for in a grocery store
- ☐ Basic questions
  - What? When? Where? Why? How? Who?
- ☐ You're welcome
- ☐ Excuse me and sorry
- ☐ Directional
  - Right, left, stop, straight, corner
- ☐ Floor
  - For directions ('3rd floor)
- ☐ Blocks or streets
  - For directions ('Three streets ahead')
- ☐ I am learning [target language]
- ☐ Today, tomorrow, yesterday
- ☐ Many or a lot of
- ☐ Numbers 0 – 9
- ☐ Here and there
- ☐ Wine
- ☐ Days of the week
  - Monday, Tuesday, Wedneday, Thursday, Friday, Saturday, Sunday
- ☐ Easy and hard
- ☐ Before and after

- ☐ Spoon, knife, fork, napkin
- ☐ Sweet and Sour
- ☐ Beer
- ☐ Breakfast, lunch, and dinner
- ☐ Pronouns
  - Me, you, he, him, her, she, it, they, us, them, we
- ☐ Prepositions
  - With, in, next to, in front of, behind, on, about, of, from
- ☐ Food names
  - Eggs, chicken, apple, fish, nuts, milk, sugar, cheese, bread, rice, etc.
- ☐ Colors
  - White, brown, yellow, orange, green, black, blue
- ☐ Second, minute, hour
- ☐ Cold, Warm, Hot
- ☐ Quiet and loud
- ☐ Soon
- ☐ Job
- ☐ Waiter(ess)
- ☐ Slow and fast

- ☐ Day, month, year
- ☐ Cheap and expensive
- ☐ Filler words
  - Because, of, or, maybe, to, the
- ☐ Emotions
  - Happy, sad, bored, overwhelmed, depressed, excited, busy, etc.
- ☐ Body parts
  - Tongue, mouth, leg, hair, eyes, hands, shoulder, neck, ear, etc.
- ☐ Months
  - January, February, March, April, May, June, July, August, September, October, November, December
- ☐ Verbs
  - To do, to go, to be, to want, to eat, to sign, to pay, to drink, to walk, to open, to meet, to close, to see, to talk, to call, to answer, to listen, to touch, to stand, to sleep, to look/watch, to sit, to buy, to wake up,
- ☐ Useful starters
  - I/You want, I/You have, I/You need, I/You am going to

Below is a list of short phrases that will be most useful to you. They're designed to ask and answer all the basics questions that a stranger may want to know. As you learn more phrases, you will start to notice patterns. You will also want to ask these questions, so be sure to know the common responses so you can continue the conversation.

The first three are the most important as they will be directly responsible for added learning in real conversation throughout the entire process.

As mentioned in previous chapter, this is the key to seeing the language from the 30,000-foot vantage point and starting to understand it before you even technically learn the rules as to why. In the end, languages DO make sense.

As always, there will be personally relevant phrases that you will add to this list. Also keep an ear out for common and unique phrases. For example, in Russian you can say 'Давайте познакомимся' (let's get acquainted) if you want to meet someone.

- ☐ How do you say X?
- ☐ How are you?
- ☐ What's your name?
- ☐ My name is [your name].
- ☐ Nice to meet you!
- ☐ I am from [your country].

- ☐ Have a nice day/weekend.
- ☐ Do you speak English?
- ☐ Can you please say it again slowly.
- ☐ Let's go.
- ☐ What does X mean?
- ☐ (Where's the) bathroom?
- ☐ How much?
- ☐ What are you doing?
- ☐ How was your weekend?
- ☐ What is your wifi password?
- ☐ What are your hobbies?
- ☐ I don't understand.
- ☐ I don't know.
- ☐ I am lost.
- ☐ I need directions.
- ☐ Where are you from?

Ideally, you want to fit your Anki deck reviews in your daily routine. For me, this means doing a few in between breaks while I'm at the gym in the morning when I otherwise would be listening to music and doing nothing else. Find your sweet spot during the day and review at that time. But, always review!

Those days when it seems so easy and preferable to skip are the days you should push through.

XI. Recommended Other Readings + Resources

As mentioned a couple times in this guide, if you're going to make another buy after this, there is a clear winner: Fluent Forever by Gabriel Wyner

But you can also check out the Fluent Forever Free Language Learning Resources (https://blog.fluent-forever.com/language-resources/). Just scroll to the bottom and select your target language. At the time of this writing, there are 16 languages to choose from.

I found www.lang-8.com useful, and it's free. The approach is mostly reading-based.

I found www.Language101.com to be unbiased for reviews of different language-learning methods and technology.

The Foreign Service Institute (FSI) (http://www.fsi-language-courses.net/) teaches languages quickly and efficiently to United States government officials and diplomats. I never went this route, because I hear it's dry and uninspiring. However, I've also heard that it works. The above link and this one, https://fsi-languages.yojik.eu/languages/fsi.html, are the two best resources I found if you don't mind this method of learning.

If you're learning Spanish, you can check out the Accelerated Spanish course by Masters of Memory (http://masterofmemory.com/accelerated-spanish-choose/).

Ok. We did it! Now you know how to learn a language. You have to tools. Go forth and learn to communicate with more of the world!

I'm truly curious what you think of this guide. Please use the contact info above to get in touch with me or leave a review. It helps tremendously!

CPSIA information can be obtained
at www.ICGtesting.com
Printed in the USA
LVHW061015250121
677417LV00027B/277

9 780999 715550